The Speckled Monster

Or How the Smallpox Vaccine was Discovered

written by Della Rowland

illustrated by Jeff Shelly

Table of Contents

**McGraw-Hill
School Division**

New York   Farmington

The Speckled Monster

For nearly 12,000 years, smallpox raged throughout the world. The virus was so widespread and so terrible that it killed millions of people. It even played a part in the downfall of at least three civilizations. Scientists have actually found Egyptian mummies with smallpox scars! Today it no longer exists, thanks to Edward Jenner, who in 1796 developed a vaccine for the virus. It was the first vaccine in history.

In Jenner's time, smallpox was the worst disease ever known. It was also very easy to contract. It could be passed from one person to another through sneezes or coughing. Someone could even catch it by simply handling some object an infected person had touched, such as clothing or a blanket. In no time at all, an entire village or town would be ill.

The virus brought on high fevers, chills, and vomiting, and itchy blisters that covered a victim's entire body. After these blisters scabbed over and healed, they left deep, sometimes terrible scars, called *pockmarks*. Because of these scars, smallpox was called *The Speckled Monster*.

People were terrified of smallpox, since nearly everyone caught it. A few cases were mild. Most were severe, with half its victims dying. Those who survived often suffered from pneumonia or heart failure. Sometimes they were left with muscle and joint aches, deafness, blindness, or brain damage.

Smallpox is a virus and there was no cure for it. Viruses, such as the common cold, cannot be cured with medicines like penicillin, which is an antibiotic. Antibiotics only cure illnesses caused by bacteria, such as strep throat.

Each time you get a bacterial infection, you have to take medicine to get better. However, if you contract a virus, the body forms its own antibodies, which are special types of proteins, to fight it off. These antibodies will then protect you from that particular virus for the rest of your life. So each time you get a cold, remember that it's different from all the others you've ever had. You will never have that particular cold again!

It was known that smallpox survivors could never catch the disease again. So sometimes people would try to catch it from someone with a mild case of it. They hoped that perhaps they too would have only a mild case and would then be immune, or resistant, to it. Others tried to inoculate, or inject, healthy people with smallpox.

Sometimes these attempts worked, though often they did not. Jenner himself was inoculated with smallpox when he was eight years old. Although he recovered, he suffered from sleeplessness and sensitivity to sudden, sharp noises for the rest of his life.

A Milkmaid's Tale

Jenner was born May 17, 1749, in Glouchestershire, England. At the age of twelve he became an apprentice to a country doctor named Daniel Ludlow. In those days, a young person normally learned a trade by working for someone who was already in that profession. Jenner's assignments were to help Dr. Ludlow give out medicines and perform certain surgical operations.

During his fourth year with Dr. Ludlow, a milkmaid came in to get a sore on her hand treated. Ludlow automatically thought it was smallpox by the way it looked.

No, the milkmaid told them. She could never have smallpox because she had already had cowpox. Cowpox was like a mild case of smallpox that people caught from cows. Milkmaids often developed it by milking cows infected with cowpox. Once the milkmaids had cowpox, however, they almost never contracted smallpox.

At that time, many people thought the connection between cowpox and smallpox was just folklore. There was no scientific proof that it was true. Jenner, however, never forgot what the milkmaid said. From that time on, he was fascinated by the possible connection between the two diseases.

In 1770, when he was 21, Jenner went off to London to study with John Hunter, a surgeon and teacher at the Windmill Anatomy School. As Hunter's assistant, he learned anatomy, natural history, and surgical techniques. Perhaps the most important knowledge Jenner learned from Hunter was how to use scientific methods. In other words, he learned how to do research. Hunter's favorite saying was, "Why think, why not try the experiment?" He meant, Why should you guess at something? Do experiments to prove it!

After two years, Jenner returned to his home in Glouchestershire to set up practice as a country doctor. By that time outbreaks of smallpox were increasing. Many authorities felt the inoculation attempts were spreading the disease rather than stopping it. A few countries, such as France, had outlawed inoculations entirely. However, Jenner had been forming his own theory about inoculation since he first met the milkmaid at Ludlow's. He was convinced that there was a connection between cowpox and immunity from smallpox. And he intended to prove it.

Proving a Theory

Jenner knew of a farmer named Benjamin Jesty. Jesty had had cowpox and remained healthy during several smallpox epidemics. Jesty had injected his wife and two sons with material he had taken from cows infected with cowpox. This did not have the same effect. Others had also carelessly tried inoculating themselves, but then gave up when something went wrong. Jenner felt he could find a successful vaccine by using organized scientific experiments.

The first thing Jenner did was to define what true cowpox was. He began making careful drawings of cowpox marks he found on cows and milkmaids during each day of the illness. These observations showed the different stages of the blisters. Then he matched them day by day and compared them.

Similar blisters often appeared on horses' heels. This horsepox could be passed to cows where it became cowpox, which was then passed to milkmaids. So Jenner began making drawings of horsepox blisters as well.

In 1791, Jenner learned of a milkmaid who had come down with smallpox even though she already had cowpox. At first Jenner was confused. Then he realized that the cowpox could be more powerful at different stages of the illness.

One person might milk a cow with cowpox on Monday, catch the disease, and then be resistant to smallpox forever. Another person might milk the same cow a day later, when the cowpox had begun to lose its strength. That person might have only the symptoms of cowpox, not the real disease, and therefore would end up not being immune to smallpox.

"Why not Try the Experiment?"

Jenner spent years drawing and comparing, and carefully recording his observations. Finally he was ready to test his theory by experimenting on people. First he injected smallpox into twelve people who had had cowpox and three who had had horsepox. When none of them got smallpox he was ready for the next stage of his research. This was a lot more dangerous—injecting a healthy person first with cowpox and then smallpox.

Today this may seem somewhat shocking. Of course this is no longer the way medical research is carried out. At the time, however, Jenner knew of no other way to test his theories. Even though some people today may be uncomfortable with Jenner's use of human subjects, we all appreciate the results of his studies.

In May 1796, a milkmaid named Sarah Nelmes developed cowpox from a cow she was milking. Jenner extracted some cowpox from her. Then he injected it into two scratches he made on the arm of James Phipps, a healthy eight-year-old. Jenner had purposely picked someone young and healthy to test his inoculation.

As expected, James came down with cowpox. It lasted only three days. Jenner waited six weeks, and then injected James with smallpox. Would the child come down with the virus? If he did, would he live? Would he be scarred for life? If that happened, it would be Jenner's fault.

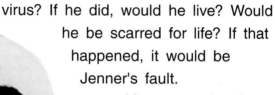

After a couple of weeks, James was still healthy. Jenner was sure his theory was working. A few months later he injected the child again and got the same result: no smallpox.

Jenner had to wait for two years to try more experiments because there were no cases of cowpox in his area. Finally, in February 1798, he heard that a mare on a nearby farm had come down with horsepox. Shortly afterwards some of the cows developed cowpox. When three men on the farm caught the cowpox, Jenner hurried there to perform the next stage of his experiment.

First he injected a healthy boy with fluid from a blister on one of the cows. When that boy came down with cowpox, Jenner took some fluid from his blisters and injected it into a second boy. After the second boy developed cowpox, Jenner drew fluid from his blisters and injected a third. Jenner continued giving injections to a series of several children and adults. Later, when these people were injected with smallpox, not one of them got it. Jenner now knew he could inoculate people with cowpox without having to get it directly from the cow.

Making Medical News

Satisfied that he now had a reliable inoculation, he wrote up his findings for England's medical society. Its members refused to publish Jenner's paper because it did not fit in with the current thinking. They still believed that inoculations were spreading smallpox rather than preventing it. Finally Jenner published his paper himself with the long title, "An Inquire into the Causes and Effects of the Variolae Vaccinae, a Disease Discovered in Some of the Western Counties of England, Particularly Glouchestershire, and Known by the Name of Cow Pox." The word vaccinae is another way of spelling vaccine. It comes from the Latin word *vaca*, meaning cow.

After his paper was published he went to London where he hoped volunteers would be eager to try his vaccination. Three months went by and no one came forward or seemed to have even heard of his vaccine. Still determined, Jenner never swerved from his goal. He located a few doctors who were willing to do inoculations and in only six months his cowpox vaccine became the talk of London.

Jenner had proven that the cowpox vaccine prevented smallpox. Yet it took ten more years for vaccinations to become commonplace. Jenner's efforts were often set back by bad publicity. This would happen when doctors did not know how to use the vaccine and would inject a healthy person with smallpox instead of cowpox.

Jenner kept busy clearing up incorrect statements made by ignorant doctors. One claimed that being injected with cowpox would turn a human into an animal. It was such a crazy idea that the newspaper cartoonists of the day drew hilarious cartoons of it.

A Vaccine that Changed History

By 1880, the vaccine was being used in most European countries. Nearly 100,000 people had been vaccinated around the world. Jenner's work laid the foundation for future scientists to find other vaccines. Though he was not the first to try inoculations, he was the first to prove his theory scientifically. He was also the first to try controlled experiments that led to a safe, effective vaccine.

Just as important were his experiments on passing cowpox from human to human, instead of from cow to human. That proved that a vaccine could be produced without the original source. This made it possible to mass-produce the vaccine.

Two hundred years after little James Phipps was first vaccinated, smallpox has been wiped off the face of the earth. In fact, no one is even given smallpox vaccinations anymore. The World Health Organization (WHO) was unsure whether or not to destroy the remaining samples of the virus that are stored in laboratories. One argument for keeping them is so that future scientists can study them. On the other hand, the possibility of someone removing smallpox from a lab would present a terrible risk to the entire world.

In 1996, the WHO recommended keeping 500,000 doses of the vaccine, and destroying all stocks of the viruses except one. This one could be used to make more vaccines, if necessary.

By the way, did you wonder what happened to James Phipps? Jenner injected him 20 times with smallpox and he never caught the disease. Instead he lived to a ripe old age in a cottage that Jenner built for him.